Really Useful Guides

Psalms

The Bible Reading Fellowship
15 The Chambers, Vineyard
Abingdon OX14 3FE
brf.org.uk

The Bible Reading Fellowship (BRF) is a Registered Charity (233280)

ISBN 978 0 85746 731 7
First published 2018
10 9 8 7 6 5 4 3 2 1 0

Cover image by Rebecca J Hall

Acknowledgements
Scripture quotations from The New Revised Standard Version of the Bible, Anglicised edition, copyright © 1989, 1995 by the Division of Christian Education of the National Council of the Churches of Christ in the United States of America. Used by permission. All rights reserved.

Every effort has been made to trace and contact copyright owners for material used in this resource. We apologise for any inadvertent omissions or errors, and would ask those concerned to contact us so that full acknowledgement can be made in the future.

A catalogue record for this book is available from the British Library

Printed and bound in the UK by Zenith Media NP4 0DQ

Really Useful Guides

Psalms

Simon P. Stocks

Contents

1

Why read the psalms? A personal reflection

When I first became enthused about reading the Bible as a teenager, I was pretty rigorous about reading my three chapters a day (five on Sunday) so that I would get through it in a year. I even stuck at it through Leviticus – though I cannot claim to have actually read every single name in those long lists! Yet the part of the Bible that I read the least carefully at that time was probably the psalms. They just didn't seem very readable. I could readily make sense of the narrative books of the Bible, and the laws and prophecies were reasonably accessible (if a little dull or obscure), but I just didn't seem to 'get' the psalms.

For many years, the psalms were not part of the worshipping tradition of the churches I attended, and so they were not explicitly in my awareness. (Only subsequently have I discovered how many songs and hymns were based on them.) I next came across the psalms when I was at theological college and we would use one as part of morning prayer each day. I can still recall how strongly I reacted day by day as the person leading would say something like, 'This morning we will say Psalm 28.' I was (inwardly) shouting 'Why?! Why are we doing that? Why are we using these strange words to express sentiments that I don't even relate to?'

In time, my bafflement found a constructive outlet, and I began my study of the psalms which has continued since. What I soon discovered was that my mindset, both as a teenager and as an adult, had been awry. The psalms are not for reading in the same way that a story is for reading, because they are much more intense and rich. They need to be experienced and felt as much as heard. It was when I slowed down and dwelt with the psalms awhile that they started to come alive. I was like someone who had only ever drunk Americano coffee, learning how to savour and appreciate a really good espresso. They require a different sort of reading.

The psalms also require a different sort of 'saying' – they really make sense when they are prayed. As a means of sharing in the faith experience of those who wrote them, the psalms really started to hit the mark when I learned to pray them with and for other people. They provide a real point of connection with God's people – past and present – who share the same joys, struggles and hopes that I do. And it is this emotional richness that has really had the most significant impact on me. Strong feelings do not always find comfortable means of expression in contemporary Christian life; indeed, some forms of Christian community can be positively averse to them. Yet, in the psalms, I have found the most extraordinary and wonderful way to connect with God through every shade of emotion.

So, I invite you to read the psalms with me: to learn to appreciate their richness, their flavours and their intensity. May they enrich your own faith and, through your praying them, that of many others too.

2

What is the book of Psalms?

Imagine 2,000 years from now, in a digital age, when only a handful of people are allowed access to old paper documents, one of the country's last ever printed hymn books (dated 2025?) is discovered. What a fascination! If you were in that situation, what would your questions be? What would you want to investigate? Perhaps which hymns/songs were included and which not; or the order in which they were printed; or the topics and ideas about God that they covered? Could they be related to anything else that was known about the Christian church in the early 21st century? All of which would be helped enormously if there was an editor's Foreword to the hymn book (as there usually is) addressing those sorts of issues.

The book of Psalms is a collection of hymns, songs and prayers from ancient Israel, originally written in Hebrew. Sadly, it does not have an editor's Foreword, but it does give us a fascinating insight into the beliefs, hopes and worship of the Israelites. And, as it was in use at the time of Jesus, it was particularly influential on the New Testament writers and on Christian traditions of devotion and worship.

The book of Psalms, also known in English as the Psalter, consists of 150 numbered psalms. As hymns and prayers, they are generally addressed to God. They have always been associated with music and being sung; several of the psalms themselves mention the use of music and singing (for example, 49:4; 92:3). Some appear to be specifically intended for congregational singing, whereas others are more adaptable to a range of contexts. The psalms vary in length very widely: the shortest (117) is just two verses, whereas the longest (119) is 176 verses.

As you read the psalms, you will find that often God and God's actions are the sole concerns of a psalm, while in other psalms there can be attention given to the psalmist themselves, to God's people generally, or to a historical figure or specific place. In a few cases, a psalm is neither addressed to God nor talks about God, but is addressed to other people as a direct means of passing on advice for good and godly living.

The Psalter is traditionally grouped into five smaller collections or 'books' of psalms: 1—41, 42—72, 73—89,

90—106 and 107—150. The division into books is identified by a concluding doxology – a short expression of giving glory to God by means of the phrase 'Blessed be the Lord...' Have a look at the end of Psalms 41, 72, 89 and 106 and you will see this. After the end of Psalm 72, you will find an extra fascinating comment! At the very end of the Psalter, the same form of expression is not used. Why do you think that might be?

This feature of the Psalter shows us that the psalms have been assembled and rearranged over a period of time, probably from other smaller collections. Moreover, the insertion of these concluding expressions of glorifying God suggests that the primary purpose of the psalms is to be a means of giving glory to God. They have their fullest meaning when we use them for that purpose. In fact, the Hebrew title for the Psalter is 'Praises'. This does not fairly reflect the variety of types of psalm found in the book, but does convey the sense that all the psalms are fundamentally for giving glory and honour to God.

Within the five 'books' of psalms, there are also some smaller collections. Many psalms (but not all) have a heading in the Hebrew text that associates a psalm with a particular character or occasion. For example, Psalms 73—83 are associated with Asaph, who was appointed the chief of the temple musicians in 1 Chronicles 16:7. And Psalms 120—134 are all headed 'Song of Ascents', which is possibly a reference to pilgrimage up to Jerusalem. You may wonder why the psalms are collected as they are, or put into the order that they are. See if you can discern any connections between psalms as you read them. Sometimes there will be, at other times not.

The headings (known technically as 'superscriptions', meaning 'written at the top') are translated and included in some English versions of the Bible, but not all. Have a look in your Bible and see if they are there. For example, the heading for Psalm 73 is 'A Psalm of Asaph'. There might be another heading in your Bible as well as (or instead of) that one. It would probably be in italics and say something like 'Plea for relief from oppressors'. This is an extra explanation of the psalm that has been added by the English translators.

The most common phrase found in the headings is 'Of David'. This has given rise to the tradition of the psalms having been written by King David, the second king over all Israel as told in the book of 2 Samuel. (Mentions of David being a musician, such as in 1 Samuel 19:9, also contribute to this tradition.) In some instances, it is clearly impossible that King David could have been the author of a psalm (see section 5 on historical context), while in others it is plausible. However, the phrase 'Of David' is particularly ambiguous in its meaning (even more so in Hebrew than in English). It could imply 'written by David' but could also mean any of the following: 'About David', 'In the style of David', 'For David', or 'In honour of David'.

Be cautious in making assumptions about how a particular psalm is related to the life of King David. It is probably helpful to use the background of King David's life to add some context and character to the psalms, but not to limit their meaning to those specific details. We can make the same point through our analogy of a modern hymn book. We might know that a hymn was written by John Wesley, and it might have had particular connection to events in his life. But the hymn will have taken on a life of its own: it will have been used for over 200 years by many people who did not know about the circumstances of its origin. Therefore, its place in the hymn book and its interpretation would not be limited by people not knowing that John Wesley wrote it, or even if it were discovered that in fact somebody else had written it.

The ambiguity in the actual author(s) of the psalms is such that we will refer to 'the psalmist' as the person who originated a particular psalm. This makes reading the psalms more straightforward and allows us to hold in our mind the various people involved in shaping the psalms, whether as authors, editors or compilers. Some of those people may be identifiable (such as David and Asaph), others not.

Thinking about human authors is part of seeing the psalms as human words expressed to God. So they originally were, and they continue to be as we read them and pray them. But as part of scripture, they are also God's word to us as we read them. So, they reveal as well as express. They make God known to us at the very moment of our reaching out to God. Or, conversely, as the great early church leader Athanasius put it, 'While most scriptures speak to us, the Psalms speak for us.' See if you can discern this two-way communication in your reading of the psalms. Where does the psalmist speak *for* you? And what does God speak *to* you?

The next two sections will delve much deeper into these two areas: What do the psalms say to us (as God's word)? And how do they say it (as a form of human expression)?

3

What do the psalms say?

Just like any hymn book, the psalms include a wide spectrum of material that defies simplistic reduction or even categorisation. Nevertheless, one particular motif runs throughout the Psalter, at times more or less explicitly. Several psalms express it very simply indeed as their opening exclamation, and it is this: the Lord is King!

Like many simple and yet profound truths, there are many different ways of saying it:

- The Lord reigns.
- The Lord rules.
- The Lord is sovereign.

Expressed so briefly, it begs all manner of questions about how the Lord rules, what sort of ruler the Lord is and what the effects of that rule are. What is your reaction to it? For some people, the concept of rule or kingship can be threatening or sinister. So, let's spell out more fully the concept and qualify it in the way that the psalms do:

1. The Lord God created everything and therefore rules over it with good will...
2. choosing Israel as a particular sign of that rule and good will...
3. using human kings as a manifestation of that rule and good will...
4. and bringing about justice in human affairs by the defeat of evil.

Hold this fundamental idea in mind as we explore the message of the psalms in their various forms.

The implications of this assertion can be worked out in the varied contours of human experience, so that it has different shades and resonances depending on the context. One way of looking at it is in the time-frames of past, present and future. We may therefore start to expand the idea a little and say that:

- The Lord has ruled in righteousness (in times past).
- The Lord rules in faithfulness (in the present).
- The Lord will ever rule in triumph (in the future).

These are not exclusive categories – we could just as well say that the Lord has ruled in triumph, and so on – but they identify a primary focus in each viewpoint that assists and orders our perspective. So, let's explore the ways in which the psalms speak of God's rule, and then develop that into the perspectives of past, present and future.

The Lord is king!

'The Lord is king!' is the opening assertion of Psalm 97. Read through this and see how it uses imagery from nature (clouds, darkness, fire, lightning) to describe the awesome might of God. As the creator of everything, God has absolute power over it, so that 'the earth sees and trembles' (v. 4). The absolute sovereignty of the Lord is emphasised by proclaiming that 'all gods bow down before him' (v. 7) and 'you are exalted far above all gods' (v. 9).

Psalm 99:1 says, 'Let the earth quake!' It goes on to more specific detail: 'The Lord is great in Zion' (v. 2), highlighting the particular significance of Zion (Jerusalem) as the location of Israel's temple. The Lord's rule is therefore particularly connected with Israel and expressed in part through its human kings who reside in Zion. There is no mention of human kings in these particular psalms, but Psalm 99:6 mentions Moses and Aaron who were God's appointed leaders of Israel before the kingship, and of Samuel who anointed kings Saul and David according to God's instruction.

The Lord's sovereignty is awe-inspiring but is also reassuring since it is used for good and for justice: 'He guards the lives of his faithful; he rescues them from the hand of the wicked' (97:10) and so is addressed as a 'lover of justice' who has 'established equity' (99:4). Such an awesome and yet wonderfully good and caring God is both worthy of great praise (99:9) and a cause for rejoicing (97:12).

1 The Lord God created everything and therefore rules over it in sovereign good will...

There are just a few psalms that speak explicitly of God's creating act and rule over creation, but these concepts are clearly underlying many other psalms too.

Psalm 104 is an extended hymn of praise, celebrating God's work in creation. In language reminiscent of the creation narrative in Genesis 1, the psalmist declares God's acts of creation:

You stretch out the heavens like a tent,
you set the beams of your chambers on the waters
you make the clouds your chariot,
you ride on the wings of the wind…
You set the earth on its foundations,
so that it shall never be shaken.

PSALM 104:2–3, 5

The psalm goes on to describe how God sustains all living creatures, which are a manifestation of God's glory. This is echoed in Psalm 65, which celebrates the fruitfulness of the earth as a gift of God:

You visit the earth and water it,
you greatly enrich it;
The river of God is full of water;
you provide the people with grain,
for so you have prepared it.

PSALM 65:9

God's glory in creation is also apparent in Psalm 8, which opens and closes with:

O Lord, our sovereign,
How majestic is your name in all the earth!

PSALM 8:1, 9

In this psalm, the specific interest of the psalmist is the ordering of creation, and the mandate given to humanity to share in God's good rule over other creatures.

The twin facets of God's awesome creative power and gentle nourishing care are also considered in extended detailed imagery. Psalm 29 focuses on the power of a storm as a manifestation of God's glory and strength, whilst Psalm 23 portrays God as a shepherd who tenderly looks after his flock. But the dominant image in the Psalter is of the Lord God as a king, who reigns supreme:

> For the Lord, the Most High, is awesome,
> a great king over all the earth...
> God is king over the nations;
> God sits on his holy throne.
>
> PSALM 47:2, 8

Which of these psalms most resonates with your understanding of God as creator? What extra insight do you get from reading them?

2 ... choosing Israel as a particular sign of that rule and good will...

The particularly important aspect of God's sovereign rule over the earth is the choice of ancient Israel – the descendants of Abraham – to have a special place and responsibility in God's purposes. The narrative of Genesis and Exodus is recapitulated briefly in Psalm 105, which identifies the Israelites as God's 'chosen ones' (105:6). Reading this psalm will give you an overview of the story that lies behind most of the Old Testament and explains how the Israelites understood their relationship with God.

The choice of Israel is not often mentioned explicitly in the psalms, but is the foundation for assertions about Israel, such as her confidence in God's protection and the special status of the city of Zion, since the temple was God's 'dwelling place' on earth:

> There is a river whose streams make glad the city
> of God,
> the holy habitation of the Most High.
> God is in the midst of the city; it shall not be
> moved;
> God will help it when the morning dawns.

PSALM 46:4–5

Besides God's presence and protection, the particular gifts of God to Israel were the land and the law: a place to inhabit as God's people plus instruction and guidance by which to live as God's people:

> He gave them the lands of the nations,
> and they took possession of the wealth of the peoples,
> that they might keep his statutes
> and observe his laws.
>
> PSALM 105:44–45

In several ways, the psalms emphasise the traditional Israelite view that God's law was a tremendously precious gift. Psalm 1 provides an ethical framework for the whole Psalter, distinguishing those who obey the law from those who are 'wicked'; Psalm 19 implicitly compares the law to the brilliant radiance and life-giving warmth of the sun; and the extraordinary Psalm 119 asserts in every way possible the value of the law and of meditation upon it. Reading these psalms can help you to recognise the value of God's word in the Bible and offer a tremendous encouragement to further reading. It is as pleasant as sunbathing!

God's plans for human life were intended to be revealed in Israel's obedience to God. An important implication of Israel's special status was its special responsibilities, so that failure to observe God's law would bring consequences. The fact of Israel's failure is readily acknowledged in the psalms; for example, in Psalm 78 you can read of Israel's persistent failures in the wilderness wanderings of the exodus.

3 ... using human kings as a manifestation of that rule and good will...

The human kings of Israel, such as King David, are given a special status and regarded as reigning on God's behalf. Their actions make known the rule of the Lord, by exercising authority and establishing justice. Therefore, some psalms assert confidence in divine aid that will ensure victory against any enemies of Israel's king:

> Now I know that the Lord will help his anointed;
> he will answer him from his holy heaven
> with mighty victories by his right hand.
>
> PSALM 20:6

Note here the identification of the king as God's 'anointed' one – the Hebrew word which comes into English as 'messiah'. Similar ideas are found in Psalms 2, 21 and 110. These are important psalms to read in order to see how ancient hopes for an anointed king allowed the early Christians to understand Jesus as that king.

In ancient Israel, the king was the key figure responsible for justice, and this forms the focus for a prayer for the king in Psalm 72:

> Give the king your justice, O God,
> and your righteousness to a king's son.
> May he judge your people with righteousness,
> and your poor with justice.
>
> PSALM 72:1–2

The supreme example of a human king was King David, and some psalms celebrate this fact and recount the promise that God made to David that he would always have a descendant as king: see Psalms 89:3–4 and 132:11–12 alongside 2 Samuel 7:8–16.

In the period of Israel's history when it did not have a human king (from the time of the exile onwards), the use of such psalms would have become future-oriented, anticipating a king or 'messiah' who was yet awaited.

4 ... and bringing about justice in human affairs by the defeat of evil

The psalms are very frank about the presence of evil and its opposition to goodness. The psalmist presumes that God is on the side of the right and will act against evil, and makes his prayer on that basis:

> Do not sweep me away with sinners,
> nor my life with the bloodthirsty,
> those in whose hands are evil devices,
> and whose right hands are full of bribes.
> But as for me, I walk in my integrity;
> redeem me, and be gracious to me.
>
> PSALM 26:9–11

In light of the evil and suffering that people experience, the psalms give particular exhortation to do what is right. You can read Psalms 26 and 37 and look out for the encouragement to do what is right, as in these verses:

> Trust in the Lord and do good;
> so you will live in the land and enjoy security.
> Take delight in the Lord,
> and he will give you the desires of your heart.
>
> PSALM 37:3–4

This encouragement is balanced by the assertion that God will act against evil in order to enact justice. In other words, God will stand against those who abuse power, privilege or wealth, but will support and help those who are weak or afflicted. In Psalm 9, this is expressed in the context of what God has already done:

> For you have maintained my just cause;
> you have sat on the throne giving righteous judgment.
> You have rebuked the nations, you have destroyed the wicked;
> you have blotted out their name forever and ever.
>
> PSALM 9:4–5

Notice that the defeat of evil by God is complete, yet ambiguous in how it has come about. The psalmist clearly relies on God as the one who can deal with evil, yet the precise details of how that happens are obscure. What is clear is that the defeat of evil is for the purpose of restoring justice and well-being to God's creation.

We have explored the basic framework of the psalms, that supposes and affirms God's good rule, expressed particularly in Israel and through Israel's king, that defeats evil and enacts justice. We can now look further at how this framework allows the psalmists to express themselves in different contexts, so that we can learn to use the psalms as prayers that express our thoughts and feelings in a variety of circumstances. We will think about past, present and future time frames.

Keeping memory alive: the Lord has ruled in righteousness

What sort of things do you say when you meet somebody for the first time? How do you help them to get to know who you are? A typical way is to give them various facts about yourself – where you are from, what you do, who else is in your family. Often this develops into telling stories, more detailed accounts of the experiences that have made you who you are. What are the stories that you would most want other people to know about you? Are there some stories that you would only tell to certain people, if you really trusted them or wanted them to know you very closely?

The people of God have always recounted facts and stories about God, to make sure that their memory of who God is remains strong and accurate. The psalms of praise are the particular way in which people have been able to express these ideas and these stories in prayer and worship. This has allowed God's people, and still allows us today, to keep our relationship with God firmly rooted in a reliable account of who God is and how God has acted in the past.

This is really important because we don't want to get the wrong idea about God. There are lots of ideas about God in the world, and we can easily get drawn in to accepting them and drifting away from who God actually is. We don't generally like it when people get the wrong idea about us. So also it is important that we don't get the wrong idea about God. The best way to avoid that is to be regularly reminded of the true understanding of who God is and what God is like.

The shortest psalm of all is a classic example of this principle. It is Psalm 117 and it expresses praise to God based on a simple assertion of what God is like:

> Praise the Lord, all you nations!
> Extol him, all you peoples!
> For great is his steadfast love towards us,
> and the faithfulness of the Lord endures
> forever.
> Praise the Lord!

That is the whole psalm! It is quite similar, in some respects, to a modern chorus: something that you might want to repeat several times, or have repeating in the back of your mind as you are doing something else. It tells us very simply and clearly what God is like – steadfast in love, faithful forever – and gives us the means to embed that in our minds by singing or praying it. So, as you read other psalms of praise, note what they tell you about God.

Other psalms of praise give more detailed descriptions of what God is like. Love and faithfulness are common themes, and these are often associated with God's justice and ruling in righteousness. Here are some verses from Psalm 33 that link these ideas together:

> For the word of the Lord is upright,
> and all his work is done in faithfulness.
> He loves righteousness and justice;
> the earth is full of the steadfast love of
> the Lord.
>
> PSALM 3:4–5

When you read the whole of Psalms, you will see how it describes God's rule, enthroned above the earth and observant of everything that everyone does. Being reminded of such ideas can be vital if we feel discouraged by what we see in the world around us. The authority of God is not always evident. When we are disturbed by the state of the world, reading a psalm of praise may be just what we need to remind us that God is faithful and continues to rule.

The faithfulness of God can be spelled out much more evocatively by telling stories about what God has done in the past. Several psalms do this; they record and affirm the fundamental acts of God's creation and deliverance of Israel, as well as less specific acts of helping and rescuing individual people. These psalms are a bit like someone giving their testimony in church, answering the question, 'What has God done in your life?' By listening in to what God has done in other people's lives, we can be encouraged that God is able to work in our life too.

Psalm 136 is a fascinating example of listing of the great things that God has done:

- created heaven and earth
- saved Israel from slavery in Egypt
- led Israel through the Red Sea
- brought them to the promised land
- rescued them from enemies
- provides food for all creatures.

And every single assertion is followed by a refrain: 'for his steadfast love endures forever'. The repetitive nature makes it a bit like a chant, that gets drummed into you until you are completely immersed in it. You could think of it a bit like a crowd at a football match. Half the crowd shouts out a list of all the trophies their team has won, and after each one the other half of the crowd shouts, 'We are the greatest!' Psalm 136 is a chant for people to be able to declare that 'God is the greatest' and to make sure that they are reminded of exactly why that is the case. Why not read it with this in mind – or perhaps even try this out in a group?

The great things that God has done in history are matched by the good things that God has done in the life of an individual. Psalm 34 is an example of someone giving thanks and praise to God because they have experienced God's help in a personal way. It is a testimony to how God has ruled in their life.

> I sought the Lord and he answered me,
> and delivered me from all my fears…
> This poor soul cried and was heard by the Lord,
> and was saved from every trouble.
>
> PSALM 34:4, 6

We are not given any specific details of the help the psalmist received here, but presumably that's not so important. In fact, it makes it helpful for us because we can readily adapt the psalm to make it our own prayer to give thanks for what God has done in our lives.

But even if we don't feel able to do that, we can stand with the psalmist and delight in the truth of God's ruling in their life. We can listen to it in the same way that we might listen to someone giving a testimony. We can be encouraged, with them, that God is in the habit of hearing people's cries and helping them.

Remembering that the Lord has ruled in righteousness tends to bring up an awareness of human failings and shortcomings. Some psalms are quite frank about this and describe the historical failings of Israel (or certain groups of people) in general. Psalm 106 recounts again the story of God's saving of Israel from slavery in Egypt and bringing them into the promised land, but with a particular focus on the disobedience and stubbornness of the people of Israel. For example:

> They grumbled in their tents,
> and did not obey the voice of the Lord.
>
> PSALM 106:25

In this telling of the story, the focus on the people's shortcomings brings into even sharper focus the goodness of God. The really encouraging aspect is that God was clearly able to cope with the people in their weakness, and showed them patience and loyalty even in the light of their rebellion. Reading Psalm 106 will show you how the memory of God's rule is a realistic one, and provides further encouragement that God is able to tolerate our failures and shortcomings.

So, we have seen how the psalms of praise keep alive the memory of God's righteous rule and ensure that our knowledge of God is maintained on a true understanding of who God is. The recounting of God's works – in the history of Israel and in individual lives – provides the secure foundation from which we can navigate whatever life throws at us. However, when life is tough, it can be hard to keep up that perspective and to hold on to the revealed truth of God's rule. At times, it doesn't seem at all as if the good and faithful God is ruling. So, when faith is tested, God's people need extra resources to help them. We'll look at those next.

Keeping faith alive: the Lord rules in faithfulness

Keeping up faith in a good and righteous God can be difficult when faced with the reality of suffering and evil in the world. It is not unusual to hear stories of people who have lost their faith or drifted away from the church as a result of suffering that they have gone through or mistreatment that they have experienced from others. Relationships break down, people hurt one another and things go wrong. This is the stuff of everyday life, so how should it affect the way we relate to God?

One response is simply to go on praising God anyway. God is still good and worthy of praise, even when evil and brokenness seem to abound. That's an admirable response if you can manage it, but clearly the ancient Israelites thought differently. Their response was to bring before God the things that troubled them with frankness and honesty, being willing to grieve and complain in their prayers and songs. The psalms that do this are known as laments and there are lots of them. Have a look at these examples:

- Psalm 3 – facing persecution
- Psalm 6 – in serious illness

- Psalm 44 – feeling abandoned by God
- Psalm 55 – when betrayed
- Psalm 80 – after a community tragedy

The psalms of lament are extraordinary prayers because of the strength of language that they use. It might seem as if they are expressing doubt in God or questioning God's good rule, but that is not the case. In fact, it is precisely a conviction that God is good and that God does rule in faithfulness which underlies the psalms of lament and drives the psalmist to cry out to God in them. Confidence in God's faithfulness is the foundation for calling upon God to act in the light of the troubles and sorrows that people experience. This will become more evident as we look at some key features of lament psalms.

The most prominent feature of the laments is that they take seriously the reality of suffering and evil. They do not shy away from it or pretend that the world is better or nicer than it really is. But they give full voice to the variety of sorrows and troubles that afflict people, including God's people.

> Be gracious to me, O Lord, for I am in distress;
>   my eye wastes away from grief,
>   my soul and body also.

> For my life is spent with sorrow,
>   and my years with sighing;
> my strength fails because of my misery,
>   and my bones waste away.
>
> PSALM 31:9–10

That is quite unlike any prayer I have ever heard in a church meeting! But it is also how some people in churches feel. It is a prayer that is frank and honest about the reality of distress and of the feelings generated as a result. The presence of such prayers in the Bible affirms those who are suffering because it shows that God's people before us have also suffered; expressing that suffering in prayer is a legitimate expression of faith.

Many laments are quite vague regarding the particular problems the psalmist is faced with; others are more specific. Among the laments there are clear references to prolonged illness, fear of death, poverty, oppression by others, betrayal by a friend, loneliness, humiliation, destruction of property and even apparent abandonment by God. But in all these situations, the description of distress and expression of lament is an act of trust in God's faithfulness, relying on God to respond. It is not merely moaning for moaning's sake.

Of course, the most severe test of faith is when it appears that God is the problem (rather than other people, illness, etc.). What if God does not respond to prayer? In such instances, the psalmist is willing even to complain to God and to ask searching questions.

> Rouse yourself! Why do you sleep, O Lord?
> Awake, do not cast us off forever!
> Why do you hide your face?
> Why do you forget our affliction and oppression?
>
> PSALM 44:23–24

In this case, the psalmist clearly believes that God is failing to protect the people and to be faithful to them. To complain in this manner might seem incredibly shocking, but it is an act of faith to do so. It is to take seriously God's promises of faithfulness and love and to rely on them: to rely on them so strongly and seriously that there is reason to question God when they are apparently not met.

One of the remarkable aspects of such prayer is that we can see how it draws the people who are suffering closer to God, enabling them to engage with God at a deep level based on the reality of their situation. Presumably this is what God would want. So read these psalms thinking about how they can help someone to pray when they are in distress. That person might be yourself, or someone you know.

The reliance on God's faithful rule, even when expressed in such lament and complaint, is all the more evident in the plea for God's help. All the psalms of lament present their distress as a prelude to seeking aid and relief from God. In doing so, they generally assert confidence in God's goodness, which is itself a form of praise. In Psalm 28 the psalmist cries out:

> Hear the voice of my supplication,
> as I cry to you for help,
> as I lift up my hands
> toward your most holy sanctuary.
>
> PSALM 28:2

... but then proclaims:

> Blessed be the Lord,
> for he has heard the sound of my pleadings.
> The Lord is my strength and my shield;
> in him my heart trusts;
> so I am helped, and my heart exults,
> and with my song I give thanks to him.
>
> PSALM 28:6–7

It cannot possibly be the case that all the psalmist's problems have disappeared in the space of saying the psalm! But his perspective has shifted somewhat as his attention has turned from his trouble. By describing and presenting his distress based on the foundation of God's faithful rule, he has been able to express fresh confidence in that rule, sure that God will respond to his prayer and help him.

So the psalm of lament is not a wallowing in self-pity nor is it a faithless thing to do. But it reveals that God knows and understands the reality of human suffering and has provided a means of prayer in situations of distress. Such prayer takes suffering seriously but also takes God's goodness and faithfulness seriously. Do you find it difficult to praise God when you are in turmoil? Praying a psalm of lament might be the thing to gently refocus your perspective from the world's brokenness to the God of healing.

Exactly how God will respond in his sovereign goodness is not always apparent, but the psalms are full of hope and expectation that God will do so at the right time. This prospect is what keeps hope alive, and we shall consider this aspect next.

Keeping hope alive: the Lord will ever rule in triumph

There are certain times when we naturally tend to look forward to the future. These are usually at the beginning of something new: a new project, a new year, a new season or a new government. At times like these, we may have various hopes and aspirations. We think about how we would like things to turn out.

There are other times when looking forward is less comfortable and hope is more difficult to generate. These are the difficult times that give rise to the psalms of lament that we discussed in the previous section. It is especially difficult to maintain hope when things seem to have gone badly wrong or when evil seems to have the upper hand. In Christian terms, this is typified by those few days between the death of Jesus and his resurrection: the awful dark moments when hope melts away.

Therefore, two important features of the psalms of lament are the expression of hopeful waiting and the prayer that God will once again have the upper hand against those who do wrong by harming others.

Psalm 130 begins with a most evocative and haunting cry: 'Out of the depths I cry to you, O Lord.' This is the prayer of someone who feels at 'rock bottom' as we might say, who is stuck in a pit from which there is no obvious way out. Have you ever felt like that? But the key message of the psalm is to wait and to have hope. It uses the image of watching through the night to express confidence that however 'dark' the situation might seem, the promise of dawn will come and is worth waiting for.

> I wait for the Lord, my soul waits,
>   and in his word I hope;
> my soul waits for the Lord,
>   more than those who watch for the morning,
>   more than those who watch for the morning.
> O Israel, hope in the Lord!
>   For with the Lord there is steadfast love,
>   and with him is great power to redeem.
>
> PSALM 130:5–7

These lines express so strongly the idea that God will once again make his rule evident and will come out on top in the end. God will 'redeem' – put things back right. Such hope for restoration is what we need to cling on to when things are at their worst. Hope of that sort can be generated by reading this psalm.

The expression of hope is often coupled with a prayer that God will act to reassert his good rule. This will inevitably involve acting against those people or spiritual forces that oppose God's rule by doing evil. Therefore, several psalms include prayers that God would fight for the psalmist against his enemies.

> For the insolent have risen against me,
> the ruthless seek my life;
> they do not set God before them.
> But surely God is my helper;
> the Lord is the upholder of my life.
> He will repay my enemies for their evil.
> In your faithfulness, put an end to them.
>
> PSALM 54:3–5

Such language can seem vindictive and inappropriate to us today. That is a topic we will return to in section 6. For now, we should simply note that this prayer is an expression of hope for the future. It is holding on to the belief that God will triumph in the end and that therefore all manifestations of evil will necessarily have to be destroyed.

Crucially, though, it leaves open the question of how that will come about. It leaves the matter in God's hands. It does not use this hope as a pretext for taking the matter into the psalmist's own hands to exact revenge on his enemies. The prayer is not, 'Please help me, Lord, to defeat these people who want to harm me' but it is, 'I am trusting you, Lord, to defeat these people who want to harm me.'

Such confidence in God to rule in triumph in the future is expressed as a belief in God as the good king, that we explored earlier.

> The Lord is king forever and ever;
> the nations shall perish from his land.
>
> PSALM 10:16

God will therefore do the things that a good king would do. Psalm 146 lists these:

- set prisoners free
- open the eyes of the blind
- lift up those who are bowed down
- watch over strangers
- uphold orphans and widows
- bring the wicked to ruin.

But this still leaves some ambiguity: exactly how will God do these things? One possibility is that God will act through a human king, who will be like David,

Israel's greatest king, and will faithfully restore God's rule. Have a look again at Psalms 2 and 110. They use language that describes a human figure ruling on God's behalf. They contribute to the book of Psalms' vision for God's future rule, and became a rich source of reflection for the New Testament writers as they considered how God was at work in and through Jesus.

We have now completed our survey of what the psalms say. The core motif that we have explored is that of God's faithful, good rule over his people. God is portrayed as a good ruler, who cares for the people and whose good intentions cannot ultimately be thwarted, although temporarily there is evil and suffering that spoil and cause trouble. We have seen that the psalms tell the story of God's actions in the history of Israel (in order to keep that memory alive); they trust God for help in times of trouble (in order to keep faith alive); and they look forward for God's future perfect rule (in order to keep hope alive). Look out for how these ideas are apparent in your reading of the psalms.

Such ideas and functions are not achieved through the statement of facts or the narration of a story in the conventional sense. Rather, the psalms do all these things as hymns, songs and poems that were written for God's people to use in their devotion and worship. They are as much for expressing as for reading. As songs and poems, they follow the conventions of poetry from the culture of the time they were written. This has some similarities to poetry that we are familiar with today, but also significant differences. Therefore, our next task is to explore the nature and style of the psalms. We have asked, 'What do they say?' Now we ask, 'How do they say it?'

4

How do they say it?

Poetic style

Every language and culture has its own particular way of making poetry. In modern English, this is most often done by the use of regular rhythm and rhyme. Traditional hymns and songs use this approach. There are well-known styles that follow a particular fixed pattern. If you are familiar with that pattern, you will know what to expect. A good example is a limerick. Here's a favourite of mine:

There was a young bear at the zoo
Who always had something to do
When it bored him to go
On a walk to and fro
He reversed it, and walked fro and to.

You may or may not find that amusing! But more importantly, if you are familiar with limericks, you will recognise the pattern of rhythm and rhyme so that you know what to expect as you read through. But if you are not familiar with limericks, it might seem quite odd. You will not know what to expect, and you might wonder why it has been written in the way that it has. This shows us that we need to have an understanding of the conventions of a particular style of poetry in order to appreciate and enjoy it.

The psalms were written many centuries ago in Hebrew, using a style that is different from most typical modern English poetry. Therefore, we need to explore Hebrew poetic style a little bit, in order to appreciate it well.

Hebrew poetry is structured through patterns of repetition and matching. Words and phrases may be repeated or matched up with similar words at key points in a poem. A classic example is Psalm 8. Look at this and you will see that it begins and ends with exactly the same sentence. You could think of this as a bit like a picture frame, which sets the context for the image within it. Similarly, key words may be repeated at different places in a poem, to mark out different sections, much as a pop song will use a chorus at the end of each verse.

The most important feature of Hebrew poetry is the way that matching is applied to each line of poetry: the text is written in couplets. In other words, rather than each line being a single piece of text, it is split into two short phrases that stand side by side. You can see this on the page in most Bibles, and in the psalm verses that have been included in this book. A verse will typically be written out in two distinct phrases, with the second phrase indented and underneath the first phrase. This shows you visibly how the poetry is structured.

These two short phrases can be matched together to make up the whole line in lots of different ways. This is what gives Hebrew poetry its sophistication and fortunately it is still apparent when the poetry is translated into English. (Patterns of rhythm and rhyme generally get lost when poetry is translated into a different language.)

Some lines say the same thing twice, but in subtly different ways. (This has a technical name: 'parallelism'.) Here's an example we have seen already:

> God is king over the nations;
>   God sits on his holy throne.

PSALM 47:8

These two phrases both describe God being a ruler, but they do so in slightly different ways. Sitting on a throne is one way of describing being a king: it represents kingship. This sort of line is not saying two different things, but it is saying one thing in two different ways. This gives more depth and detail to the image that is being expressed. I like to think of it as a 'stereo' image, having much more texture and interest than a 'flatter' single statement. It turns a 2D image into 3D. It invites you to read each part of the line in the light of the other part, so that you generate more ideas about what it means to say that God is king.

Sometimes the second part of the line does not fully repeat the idea in the first, but adds some extra detail to it. It elaborates on a particular aspect or defines a detail more specifically. Again, here are examples that we have already seen:

> I wait for the Lord, my soul waits,
>   and in his word I hope.
>
> PSALM 130:5

> You visit the earth and water it,
>   you greatly enrich it.
>
> PSALM 65:9

> I sought the Lord and he answered me,
> and delivered me from all my fears.
>
> PSALM 34:4

In each of these examples, the second part of the line elaborates or explains some aspect of the first part, or specifies a detail more exactly.

In other instances, the two parts of the line are both incomplete and need to be put together in order to make any sense, such as this one:

> I was glad when they said to me,
> 'Let us go to the house of the Lord!'
>
> PSALM 122:1

The first part of this line alone is obviously incomplete, thus creating an impetus to keep reading and see how it is completed in the second part of the line.

So, we see there are lots of different ways to relate the two parts of a couplet. But you can never tell how the parts of a particular couplet are going to be related in any one instance. This means that reading each line involves your participation: as you read the first part of each line, you know that there will be a second part, but you don't know how it will relate. So, you are drawn into the task of working out how each couplet works as you read through it. Have a look again at the examples above or read some other psalms to see what I mean.

Finally, you may have already noticed that there are a few exceptions: lines that are triplets rather than couplets. These are part of the variation of style that typifies almost all poetry, and suggests that there might be something distinct about that particular line. With three parts to the line, the possibilities for how they relate to each other are even greater than for couplets. Triplets can be used to provide emphasis or to mark out the beginning or ending of a poem or section of a poem.

Repetition and matching, in various ways, comprise the style of Hebrew poetry and give it its structure. But like any form of poetry, it also uses language quite pictorially and non-literally. Next, we will explore some of those key images, together with particular Hebrew uses of terminology.

Imagery and idiom

Like most poetry, the psalms use a lot of imagery. They do not refer to everything literally, but often describe people and ideas in terms of something else. They use figurative language. Some of these figures of speech are quite common, and not dissimilar to modern English. Look up the examples to see how they work in specific instances:

- A 'way' or a 'path' denotes lifestyle, especially the decisions that are made about how to live in relation to other people (Psalm 1).

- 'Trees' often represent life, growth and fruitfulness – the production of something good and nourishing (Psalm 1 also). The 'cedars of Lebanon' were very tall, strong and valuable trees and so are particularly representative of those characteristics (92:12).

- 'Water' can have opposing connotations: either as something nourishing and life-giving, usually when denoted as 'river' or 'dew' (36:8); or it can be threatening and chaotic when denoted as 'sea' or 'deeps' (65:7).

- 'Leviathan' and 'Rahab' are mythical creatures that represent evil or chaos and which dwell in the sea (74:14 and 89:10).

- A 'rock' is often a symbol of strength and security (19:14). In contrast, the 'earth shaking' represents calamity or serious threat, much as we might speak today of an 'earth-shattering event' (82:5).

- A 'trap' or 'snare' is usually not literal in the psalms, but represents a situation that is sinister or malicious and threatening or harmful (124:7). In contrast, safety and good will are found in a 'refuge' (14:6).

- Safety and security are also denoted by being 'in the shadow of God's wings', which draws upon the image of a bird protecting her young close to her body (17:8).

- Perhaps most fundamentally of all, 'up' and 'high' represent better/happier/more valuable/more alive (113:4), while 'down' and 'low' are the opposites (116:6).

The symbolic use of 'up' and 'down' is embedded in the ancient Israelite way of thinking about the universe. This incorporates some important principles and theological ideas which explain some of the strange language that the psalms use about the world. The Israelites would have thought of the earth as flat (just like all people at that time) and conceived the universe in layers, as shown in this diagram:

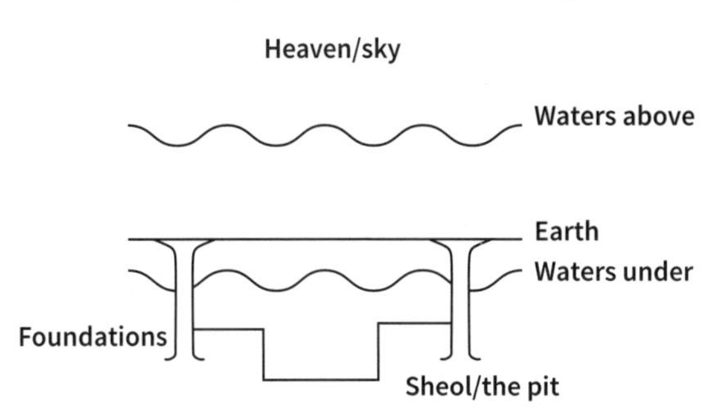

There are waters above the earth – where rain comes from – and waters below the earth – as seen in the sea. The highest level, above the waters above the earth, must be the realm of God, since God is the 'highest', the most important, most powerful. This is referred to as 'heaven', and in Hebrew the word used is the same word that is used to refer to the sky. We tend to translate differently into English according to context, but in Hebrew, 'heaven' and 'sky' are the same thing. (In Hebrew, the word appears as a plural.

This is a linguistic quirk, and is why many English translations of the Bible use the term 'heavens' rather than 'heaven'.)

The Israelites were also open to there being other divine beings, albeit always subservient to the Lord God. These beings would also dwell in 'heaven' and so there is occasionally a reference to the 'divine council'.

God is the source of life and so, within this symbolic thought-world, the more alive you are, the 'higher' you would expect to be and the closer to God. By contrast, then, death is something that takes you down and further away from God. Thus, there is an underworld which is the realm of the dead. This is known by the name Sheol, and is also sometimes referred to as the 'pit', evoking images of the grave. Indeed, burying the dead in a grave is itself suggestive of the dead person going 'down' to the underworld. It is not entirely clear whether the Israelites had an understanding of afterlife; if they did, it would certainly have involved being drawn 'up' from the world of the dead and being brought back closer to the life-giving God.

Since there was no clear or developed understanding of afterlife, the ancient Israelites were particularly concerned with justice within people's lifetimes – hence the predominant ethical perspective of the psalms is that righteousness and godliness would be rewarded and evil would be punished within a person's earthly life.

Where ideas of 'judgement' appear, we need to understand them in this context. They are not to do with declaring an individual person innocent or guilty. Rather, the role of the judge in this context would be to settle disputes between two people. Typically, one person who was weaker/poorer/less powerful would be seeking the help of the judge to stand up for them against someone else who was stronger/richer/more powerful. This is the type of 'judge' that God is portrayed as, the primary concern being to establish justice by protecting the weak and maintaining an equitable society.

Rather like the idea of a 'judge', some words and phrases are used in the psalms that refer to a real person/place/thing, but which also have symbolic significance. As before, you can look at the specific examples to see how this works:

- Jerusalem/Zion/holy hill/holy place/God's house/temple/sanctuary – these are all alternative ways of drawing attention to the temple in Jerusalem. This was considered the one place on earth where the presence of God (who dwells 'in heaven') could be experienced (Psalm 122).

- Moab, Edom and Philistia are real nations surrounding ancient Israel, but also symbolise particular threats or detestable practices (Psalms 60 and 108).

- Tarshish might be a real place, but is more important symbolically as somewhere that is a very long way away (72:10).

- The 'land' (of Israel) represents God's gift to the people and calls to mind the whole story of their deliverance from slavery in Egypt and being chosen for a special relationship with God (37:11).

- Similarly, the 'law' denotes all the instructions given by God to the Israelites so that they might live as God's chosen people. It is seen as a gift and a delight, not a burden (19:7–11). It is strongly associated with God having entered into a covenant with the people of Israel – a mutually binding commitment to each other that enmeshes their interests. God's commitment to the covenant is characterised by 'steadfast love'/'loving kindness' (17:7).

- The 'sacrifices' were the offerings (of animals and other produce) made to God in accordance with the 'law', and call to mind God's willingness to forgive and make right (66:15).

We also need to note some idioms in the Hebrew language that could easily be misinterpreted if we read them literally or according to the way the same words are used in English. An idiom is a non-literal use of language which has a commonly accepted meaning.

A common English example is: 'It's raining cats and dogs.' This is a conventional English way of saying, 'It's raining very heavily.' If you were to translate it literally into another language, it would sound like nonsense, as if cats and dogs were falling from the sky. But other languages also have idioms for heavy rain which sound like nonsense when translated into English. For example, the French say, 'It's raining ropes.'

When you read the examples of these idioms, it is important to understand them as Hebrew idioms, not as English expressions with their usual English meaning:

- 'Clean' or 'pure' means to be in right standing before God (24:4).
- 'Bones' usually refers to physical strength (51:8).
- 'Break the teeth' means to render harmless (3:7).
- 'Heart' refers not to a person's feelings but to their will and decision-making (125:4).
- 'My soul' is a poetic way of saying 'myself', with particular emphasis on being a living person (16:9; Psalm 42). It is not referring to an 'inner part' of me, distinct from my body or mind.

Finally, in some English Bibles you will come across the word 'selah' occasionally. This is a Hebrew word that nobody knows the exact significance or meaning of. It was probably some sort of indication of the structure or musical arrangement of a psalm, perhaps showing where a pause should occur or where the music rises in pitch or volume. So, it cannot be translated into English, and in many English Bibles is omitted altogether.

We have explored the poetic style of the psalms, and we have looked at the way in which they use language in a figurative and idiomatic way. Those two features relate closely to another fundamental aspect of poetry, which is that it commonly expresses feelings rather than facts. Let's reflect on this now, to make sure that we relate to the expression of the psalms appropriately.

Force and feelings

Occasionally I have had the experience of listening in on an argument between two other people in a public place. I have heard people say some quite shocking things about each other. If I took those comments at face value, I would conclude that the two people were very unpleasant and unkind people. However, I do not draw that conclusion because I recognise what is going on. I realise that feelings are running high, and that two people who are struggling with some personal distress are expressing that in an argument. The impression each person generates about the other person will inevitably be one-sided, and the other person would probably be quick to say that it was not a fair picture of who they really are. Indeed, that might well be what the argument is about!

It is helpful to hold that idea in mind as we read the psalms, since we are, as it were, listening in on a conversation between the psalmist and God. In fact, in many respects we have only one side of the conversation – the psalmist's – so it is more like listening to someone having a conversation on their phone and hearing only what they are saying, not what the person on the other end is saying. These conversations of the psalmist are often from situations of great distress, and so we should always bear that in mind when we read the psalms and consider what they mean for us.

The psalms reveal truth to us, but we need to be careful in thinking about how that truth is expressed. If poetry is primarily concerned with expressions of feelings rather than facts, we should not read the psalms as necessarily 'factual', as if everything in them is categorically correct. A good example is a text that we have already looked at: 'Rouse yourself! Why do you sleep, O Lord?' (44:23). I don't think it is appropriate to conclude from this verse that God was (or indeed ever could be) 'asleep'. For a start, figurative language is being used rather than literal. But more importantly, the psalmist, in his desperation, is saying that it feels like God is asleep, that God is ignoring him. This was, no doubt, a genuine and true feeling for the psalmist, as it continues to be for people of faith from time to time still today.

Therefore, the truth of the psalms is not always a truth that is expressed in 'facts'. Instead, like a love song or a blues song, the psalms express the truth of deep and strong feelings that are presented in figurative language, always in a way that is relevant to a particular context.

Both the exuberance of praise and the cry of lament can best be understood in this way. They are a model of 'true' and honest relating to God through the varied seasons of life. They provide a model of a person of faith engaging with God through the full extent of their being: thoughts and feelings, certainties and doubts, clarity and wrestling, all mixed up together.

This has particular significance when we come to the parts of the psalms of lament that say quite nasty things about other people. Here's an example:

> For the sin of their mouths, the words of their
>   lips,
>   let them be trapped in their pride.
> For the cursing and lies that they utter,
>   consume them in wrath;
>   consume them until they are no more.
>
> PSALM 59:12–13

To 'consume' in this context is an image of destruction, and the psalmist is effectively praying for the death of his enemies. This is sometimes referred to as 'cursing' or 'imprecation'. It is quite shocking to Christian ears, and many people are rightly very uncomfortable with even reading, let alone praying, such words. In light of that, let us simply note two things:

- The psalmist was expressing how he felt. His 'enemies' were 'evil' and 'bloodthirsty' people who were ruining his life and celebrating their apparent impunity. No wonder the psalmist felt the way he did! So we should not read the psalm as saying that the 'enemies' ought to die or that they deserved to die, but primarily as the prayer of a desperate person who felt like he wished they were dead.

- The psalmist asks *God* to deal with his 'enemies'. He does not take the matter into his own hands by asking God to help him to take his own vengeance. Instead, he asks God to take the initiative and to deal with these people. Here is a profound truth being expressed indirectly: that justice and punishment are God's responsibility. The psalm expresses a hope in God's justice, and actually pulls away from a scenario where every wronged person seeks their own vengeance.

Given what we've said about feelings vs. facts, how are the psalms 'God's word' and thus having authority? God speaks to us through these psalms in that they provide us with a model and a means of praying to God in various circumstances. Like all biblical texts, they have been produced by people under God's inspiration, and God has prompted the people of faith who went before us to include them in the Bible.

So, they do not have to be thought of as 'factual' simply because they are 'God's word'. Rather, they are a gift from God that convey truth: in this instance, the truth of human feelings and the truth of how to rightly express those feelings to God. By carrying the authority of being God's word, the psalms are 'authorised' forms of prayer, so to speak.

Such authority that the psalms have is bound up in their origin and use by particular people in particular contexts. Let's look at the context from which the psalms arose, because we need to take account of how our own context is different when we read them and pray them.

5

What was going on at the time?

A bit of history, people and places

The psalms fit within the story of ancient Israel as it is narrated in the other books of the Old Testament. The first book of Samuel tells how the Israelites first appointed a king over them, having previously been a federation of tribes. The first king was Saul; he was followed by David and then David's son, Solomon. These events are set in the tenth century BC.

During the reigns of David and Solomon, the kingdom expanded considerably, mainly through military conquest. It was relatively stable and prosperous. This was interpreted as an indication of God's blessing and was particularly associated with the idea of David being a righteous and godly ruler.

After the death of Solomon, 1 Kings tells how there was conflict over the succession, resulting in a rebellion, and the kingdom was split into two. Ten tribes rebelled against the new king (Rehoboam, son of Solomon) and appointed their own king. They formed the 'kingdom of Israel' to the north, in the areas of Galilee and Samaria. Samaria was its capital.

The other two tribes formed the 'kingdom of Judah', to the south, around Jerusalem and adjacent to the Dead Sea. Its capital was at Jerusalem, where the temple was. As we have noted above, the temple was regarded as the one place where God's presence could be experienced on earth, and thus the only right place for offering worship. At least, that was the opinion of the people of the southern kingdom, who were thus suspicious of worship offered at shrines in the northern kingdom (at places called Bethel and Dan).

The prosperity and security of these two kingdoms gradually diminished over the following three centuries, as they came under threat from neighbouring empires. The sequence of military defeats, and the eventual humiliation of destruction of capital cities, is narrated in the Old Testament as an indication of God's judgement on the two kingdoms for their failure to live according to ways that God had instructed them.

The northern kingdom fell first, being overrun by the Assyrians in 722BC. Most of the people of the northern kingdom were taken into exile, although some remained. About 130 years later, the Assyrian empire had itself been taken over by the Babylonian empire. Jerusalem fell to the Babylonians in about 586BC. Most of the wealthy were taken into exile, while the poor remained in or around Jerusalem to work the land, but under the rule of the Babylonians.

The psalms were mainly composed by the people of the southern kingdom of Judah, although some elements probably derive from the northern kingdom. The earliest might have origins as far back as the time of King David; the latest were composed during the exile in Babylon. This setting for the psalms results in many of their key themes:

- Celebration of Jerusalem and of the king
- Confidence in God's blessing the people if they follow God's ways
- Asserting God's judgement against neighbouring nations who oppose the Israelites
- Crying out in desperation when they are under threat or have actually suffered defeat and exile.

The history of the nation that lies behind the psalms sets the backdrop for them. The psalms are the hymns, prayer and songs that they sang as they lived out the story of being God's people. They had much to celebrate and enjoy, but also had to respond to terrible disasters and humiliation at the hands of others. Through it all, the fundamental perspective was that God was their good ruler, and so all their experiences were worked out in the light of that perspective.

In light of this history, how closely connected are the psalms to the precise details of events and people?

Tailor-made or made for tailoring?

Hymns and worship songs are sometimes written for a special occasion. Having a specially written song is part of the celebration. Usually, that song then passes into general use. After a while, there will be people singing it who will be unaware of the occasion for which it was written. Indeed, they might begin to associate it with a quite different context.

For example, I wrote a hymn as part of a church's celebration of its centenary. The hymn was used at the main centenary event, but then was also used afterwards. Anybody coming along later might not realise the origin of it. In fact, the hymn could potentially be used to celebrate the centenary of any Christian organisation. If it were used in that way, there would be people who then associated it with the particular event where they first heard it, without knowing that it originally belonged to the centenary of the church for which it was written.

Hold those ideas in mind as we reflect further on the historical context of the psalms. As we noted, many of them are associated with David and have a heading ('superscription') that links the psalm with a particular incident in his life. However, there is no other evidence that the psalms were necessarily written by David (or about David), and some of the details in the psalms clearly post-date David and could not possibly have been written by him or about him. Indeed, most of the wording in most psalms is very general, without any detail that could tie it to a particular place or time.

So, the question in a nutshell is this: were the psalms tailor-made, written about and for specific situations? Or were they made for tailoring, written in general terms so that they could be used and applied in many subsequent ways? The best answer we can come up with is this: probably a bit of both.

Some psalms, or parts of psalms, might well date back to the time of David and have some association with him. However, these psalms would have been edited and used in different ways over the centuries. Remember that there is a period of at least 500 years between the time of David and the compilation of the Psalter as we have it now. A lot happens in that time-span – no hymn book lasts that long! Certain traditions would have emerged over time that associated particular psalms with incidents in David's life, and these are evidenced in the psalm headings.

But the use of the psalms continued to evolve and was not limited to a recounting of David's life. Rather, they were used and applied to lots of circumstances, and the collections of psalms would continually be reshaped according to the changing needs of the community at the time. And there might well have been writers who formed new psalms over the centuries, some of which would be prompted by a particular event, and others of which would have been written deliberately generally.

Therefore, we can interpret psalms in the light of the particular events of David's life that they are associated with. Equally, we can interpret them much more generally, recognising that they would have been adapted and used in a wide variety of contexts. The remaining challenge for us, therefore, is to think about how we can apply the psalms to our own contexts today.

6

Reading the psalms today

Songs have a life that extends way beyond what was intended when they were written. A classic example is Elton John's song 'Candle in the wind', which was about the life of Marilyn Monroe. However, after the death of Diana, Princess of Wales, in 1997, the song was very movingly used at her funeral (with a tiny change to one of the lines). For many people since then, that song will be associated with Diana. Indeed, some people might even say that it is *about* Diana, even though that was never the intention when it was first written.

This dynamic worked because the song was applied to a person who was appropriate. There was a clear understanding of the sentiment of the song, and a recognition that it 'fitted' with the new circumstances to which it was being applied. It would not seem right, by way of a silly contrast, to use the same song to mark the retirement of a brash, arrogant heavyweight boxer.

Similarly, we read psalms today in contexts that were unimaginable to the people who wrote them and used them centuries ago. The matters that come naturally to our minds when we read the psalms are certainly not what the psalms were written about. But they are what the psalms are about as far as we are concerned. As we read the psalms today, we should:

- make sure that we understand them reasonably well, and then
- think about what is an appropriate way to apply them to contemporary situations.

We have already noted that the psalms are adaptable, so we can be confident that it is reasonable to apply them to new situations. But in doing so we must guard against making them mean whatever we want them to mean.

Personal reading of the psalms

Personal reading of the psalms is most typically in a devotional context. There are lots of good resources for personal devotions based on the psalms, and many people use them as part of their personal prayer life. Here's some suggestions for how to go about reading or praying a psalm:

- Try to identify what sort of psalm it is: what was the psalmist praying for/about? Skim through the psalm quickly and see if you can readily identify the key issue, and whether it is primarily a prayer of praise, or lament, or something else. Is there a topic that gets mentioned more than once?

- Look at the layout of the text on the page/screen and see if there is a structure, a division into sections. If there is, allow this to influence how you read it, pausing at the breaks between sections and being ready for a change in topic or mood.

- Read through the psalm quite slowly and see if you can discern how the thought of the psalm develops. Remember that the language of psalms is poetic: rich in imagery and at times quite dense.

- Don't worry if any details don't make sense, but keep going slowly and allow time to chew it over. The overall sense of the psalm will hopefully be apparent. Some of the ancient language is quite strange, so don't be put off by this.

- Try to imagine what might have been the original situation of the psalmist. In what context might this prayer have been offered? How might the psalm fit within the Old Testament story of the people of Israel?

- Remember that the psalm is an expression of feeling more than a statement of ideas. Aim to have sympathy with the psalmist – understanding his feelings – as much as trying to understand his thoughts and ideas.

- Focus your thinking about your own situation and discern whether there is anything similar or comparable to what the psalmist describes. If there is, then you can use the psalm to shed light on your own situation and feelings. The psalm might be an appropriate way of giving voice to your feelings or praying to God about the situation in question. Equally, the perspective of the psalm might prompt you to reappraise your own perspective on your circumstances.

- If the psalm does not relate to you personally, consider whether the psalm can be prayed on behalf of others, or read from the perspective of others. For example, carefully reading a psalm of a suffering person is a good way to identify with the experiences of people who are suffering; and praying such a psalm on their behalf can be a powerful way of praying for them, especially when it seems very difficult to know how to do so.

By spending time with a psalm and reading it slowly in this manner, I hope that it will come alive to you. Even so, it can still be challenging to discern what is appropriate when it comes to applying a psalm to our own situation. Here are some extra principles that should help with the most common issues that arise:

- In the ancient world, there was a much stronger connection between an individual person and the community to which they belonged. Therefore, there are lots of ways of identifying the person praying a psalm: the 'I' or 'me' of the psalm. They might be an individual person, but equally they might represent a whole community, standing for each individual within it.

    - Therefore, it is fine to apply an individual psalm to a whole church community, or to apply a communal psalm to a particular person. And as we noted above, even when you read a psalm as an individual, you do not have to think of the 'I' as yourself, the person reading, but could also identify with someone else and read or pray it from their perspective.

- A psalm is not usually a mandate and instruction for action. Occasionally a psalm is addressed to its hearers/readers, for example with instructions to be wise or to worship God. We will do well to heed these instructions, as part of God's word to us. But when the psalmist expresses a desire for God to do something, we should not automatically take that as an instruction for us to do it.

- The fundamental assumption of the ancient Israelites, as expressed in the psalms, is that God rules. As Christians, we still say the same, but our understanding of how God rules has developed. In particular, we now say that God rules the world in and through Jesus Christ. God's rule was evident in Jesus during his lifetime, and continues to be evident in the life of the church. But God's rule will not be fully enacted until Jesus Christ returns.

    - This has important implications for our hope for justice. The ancient Israelites probably had quite a strong sense of expecting God to deliver justice during their lifetimes. In contrast, the Christian hope calls for patient endurance, on the basis that God's retribution and defeat of all evil is delayed until Jesus Christ's return. Therefore, any psalms that seek God's action against evil must be prayed both in hope that God will respond, but also in patient waiting, not knowing when that will be.

- Where a psalm talks about 'enemies' or 'foes', there are a wide variety of ways in which we can interpret that as someone or something that makes our life difficult, threatens us or challenges our faith. It is possible to think about 'enemies' as spiritual, figurative or real. But the really important thing to note is that the psalmist surrenders retribution to God and does not take it into his own hands. The psalmist does not ask God to help him to deal with his enemies. Rather he asks *God* to deal with his enemies. (There are just one or two instances that seem to assume that the Israelites might literally fight against other nations, but that is bound up with the particular historical context of the Israelites at the time, and cannot reasonably be applied to any human situation today. See 144:1–2; 149:6–9.)

    - So, we need not think that the psalms are 'vengeful'; in fact, they are obedient and subservient to God's notions of justice. The mandate of Jesus to 'love your enemies' and 'pray for those who persecute you' may well be exercised by praying the psalms. What better thing could we do for our enemies than to place them into God's hands, who alone knows what is best and who alone rules in righteousness and justice? If we *feel* bitter and vengeful towards our 'enemies', it is far better that we bring this to expression in the God-given words of the psalms, than that we try and deal with it ourselves.

Reading a psalm in corporate worship

Whether in church or in a small group, there is a particular responsibility on behalf of the person leading worship to address some of the issues discussed in this section. It is always a good idea for a psalm to be introduced with a brief comment about how it is being used, in order to shape its interpretation. And language that superficially conflicts with a Christian perspective should be presented with some explanation of what it means in a Christian context.

7

Some specific examples

Psalm 13

Reading Psalm 13, it is clearly a psalm of lament, the prayer of someone who feels they are suffering quite badly. 'Sorrow in my heart all day long' (v. 2). This is an ongoing, chronic situation and those haunting questions really emphasise the chronic nature of the distress, 'How long, O Lord? How long?' What do you think that situation might be?

Evidently, the psalmist is ready and willing to be open and strident in describing his situation. There is no shyness or reticence here about being frank. The psalmist is only too willing to say, 'I'm in a bad way.' He knows that something is wrong; he goes straight in with the way that he feels: 'How long must I bear pain in my soul, and have sorrow in my heart all day long?' (v. 2) But more than that, he holds God to account: 'How long, O Lord? Will you forget me forever?' (v. 1).

But as you read on, there are no specific details of the psalmist's situation or what is troubling him. Whatever it is, he interprets it as an indication that the Lord God has forgotten him, the implication being that if the Lord was paying attention to him, surely he would do something about this difficult situation. The fact that it is going on and on and nothing is happening, to the psalmist, means that God must have forgotten him! So, he cries out, 'How long, O God? Will you forget me forever?'

What is your reaction to that? For many of us, it is rather shocking! Would you ever pray to God in that manner? Here it is in scripture: this is God's word to us. God has given us a mandate to use these words by putting them in scripture, reassuring us that it is okay with God for us to answer back, so to speak, and for us to say to God, 'It feels like you've just left us. It feels like you don't care. It feels like you're not there.' If that is what it feels like, the fact that God has given us these words to use means, surely, that that is okay with God. God can cope with that.

Such willingness to make the complaint, to question God and to say to God, 'Where are you?', is to depend upon and rely upon the promises that God had already made. God had declared, 'I am gracious and compassionate, slow to anger and abounding in faithful love. You will be my people and I will be your God' (see Exodus 34:6 and Leviticus 26:12). Trusting and believing such promises, the psalmist is bold to question, 'What's going on?'

In our Christian context, we should be mindful to remember that Jesus never said, 'Every little thing's gonna be alright.' That was Bob Marley, not Jesus! Jesus said, 'Whoever wants to come after me must take up their cross and follow me' (Matthew 16:24); in other words, 'I am walking in the way of suffering and anyone who wants to be my disciple must expect to suffer also.' So it cannot be the case that anything that goes wrong in life is an indication that God has forgotten us.

Nevertheless, we are legitimated in crying out to God when we are in distress because this is what God's people have always done. In the psalms of lament, we are encouraged to cry out to God when we are in distress or when others who we care about are in distress. It is an expression of faithfulness. To cry out to God and even to complain to God is one way of saying, 'God, I depend on you. You are my help and that's why I'm looking to you. I'm crying out to you because you are the only one who can sort this out.'

If you long for some chronic suffering to be alleviated, this is a prayer to use, whether for yourself or for someone else you care about.

The psalmist expresses anger to God precisely because he knows that is the safe place to take it to; because he knows that God can tolerate his anger, that God understands his human frailty and that God will not be offended. This psalm models an expression of God-focused complaint: to say how we feel and to direct it to God because God knows and God cares and God can cope with it. God is the one on whom we depend.

The psalmist goes on in the end of verse 2, 'How long shall my enemy be exalted over me?' And then he makes his prayer to God:

> Consider and answer me, O Lord my God!
> Give light to my eyes, or I will sleep the sleep of death,
> and my enemy will say, 'I have prevailed';
> my foes will rejoice because I am shaken.
>
> PSALM 13:3–4

The primary concern of the psalmist here is this concept of the 'enemy' or 'foe'. He never actually says who this person is, or what this thing is. That is helpful for praying the psalms today because we can be imaginative in how we understand the language.

Occasionally, we may have an enemy: a person who opposes us, harms us or makes life difficult for us. But a lot of the time, we may also have an enemy which is something more abstract. It may be a disease or an injury that is our enemy. We may feel that it is old age, our failing body or financial difficulty. Or we might interpret the enemy as a spiritual force of evil: that which opposes God's purposes in the spiritual realm. What would your 'enemy' be if you were praying this psalm?

After the complaint, 'Will you forget me forever?', and the naming of the trouble, 'sorrow in my heart all day long', the concern about the enemy is wrapped up with a petition that God would do something and respond: 'Consider and answer me, O Lord my God!' (v. 3). Then we find this remarkable expression:

> But I trusted in your steadfast love;
> my heart shall rejoice in your salvation.
> I will sing to the Lord,
> because he has dealt bountifully with me.
>
> PSALM 13: 5–6

This exemplifies that remarkable feature of the psalms of lament that, no matter how strident they are, no matter how whingy they are, no matter how deep the distress, they virtually *always* end up in a place where they are saying something about God's praiseworthiness or expressing some sort of trust in God.

In some ways, that should not surprise us too much from what we have already said, because the crying out to God, the laying the responsibility at God's feet is itself an expression of trust of God. Saying 'I trust in your unfailing love' is just another way of interpreting what has already gone on. There is not necessarily any change of mood at this point in the psalm, and so this is perhaps praise through gritted teeth.

Praise is *not* to do with how we feel. Praise is acknowledging and giving God the glory that is due to God because of who he is – nothing to do with who we are. This psalm belongs in a place where we are in distress, but within that situation it gives us the words to praise God: to express God's goodness and say that we will, at some point, sing to the Lord once again, even if it is not today or tomorrow. We know that is going to happen eventually and we are going to keep looking forward to it; no matter how hard it is today, we keep looking forwards to the day when we will sing with joy again.

When you are in distress, if you try to ignore your distress and praise God, the distress will remain. But if you first of all express your distress, it may just be that you find some relief from it and expressing your distress is what leads you to praise. See whether following the pattern of the laments does that for you. Try Psalm 13 in any long-term situation, or some of the other laments mentioned in chapter 3.

Psalm 30

When we have been spared a terrible fate, it is natural to want to give thanks to God. That is what is happening in Psalm 30. Its opening shows it is the prayer of someone who is giving thanks in the aftermath of recovery from an awful situation. Have you had an experience where such a prayer would be fitting? Read it through with that in mind.

> O Lord my God, I cried to you for help,
> and you have healed me.
>
> PSALM 30:2

The psalmist's situation must have been very serious, because he uses the language of 'Sheol' and 'the pit' – the world of the dead. Indeed, taken superficially, we might think that he is saying that he has been brought back to life from the dead: 'O Lord, you brought up my soul from Sheol' (v. 3). However, given the poetic nature of the text and the way similar phrases are used elsewhere, this is probably simply an exaggerated way of saying, 'You have saved me from death.' The psalmist had felt that he was 'as good as gone', and so being restored to health is presented as being 'spared from death'.

The consequence of being so close to death and then recovering is to thank God. The psalmist does this himself in verse 1 – 'I will extol you, O Lord' – and then calls upon others to do so in verse 4 – 'Sing praise to the Lord, O you his faithful ones.' From the perspective of his renewed health, he is able to reflect on his experience and recognise the relative brevity of his suffering: 'Weeping may linger for the night, but joy comes with the morning' (v. 5). This is quite a sharp contrast from the perspective of someone in the midst of suffering, for whom it seems to go on far too long, as we saw in the agonised 'How long?' questions of Psalm 13.

Throughout his experience, the psalmist knows that God has been in charge: 'For his anger is but for a moment; his favour is for a lifetime' (v. 5). The psalmist sees his suffering as God's 'anger', and his recovery and health as a manifestation of God's favour. This perspective might sit uncomfortably with us today, and probably rightly so. It is not very nice to tell someone who is gravely ill that God is 'angry' with them. But, from the perspective of the psalmist, it is a way of acknowledging that all of life is under God's sovereignty. God alone gives life and sustains it. Health is indeed a gift from God, and suffering can only persist if God allows it to. How does this affect your perspective on your own experience?

In the second half of the psalm, there is a summary account of the events leading up to this prayer of thanksgiving. The psalmist was prosperous, comfortable and well, and confident of God's favour and protection (vv. 6–7a). He perhaps admits that he was a bit over-confident. Then something happened that brought with it the real prospect of death; this is explained as God 'hiding his face' (v. 7b), an expression used throughout the Old Testament to mean the withdrawal of God's immediate care and protection. Therefore, the psalmist cried out to God (vv. 8–10) and sought again God's gracious help. Having received that help, he recounts how mourning has turned into dancing (v. 11), and acknowledges a duty to praise God. The psalm concludes with an exaggerated flourish, vowing to give thanks to God 'forever' (v. 12).

This brief cameo of a person who experiences sudden disaster but then recovers is fascinating because it reflects common life experiences on many levels. You could reflect on your own experiences of life 'going wrong' in some respect and then later being set right. The variety of types of psalm that we have examined earlier fit into different phases of that cycle:

- Feeling settled and confident is the context in which the hymns that praise God's dependability belong. We are readily able to assert God's goodness and faithfulness when life reflects those truths.

- When things go wrong, that confidence can be shaken. Then the primary mode of relating to God becomes one of lament and petition, wrestling with the apparent incongruity between God's goodness and the distress in which we find ourselves. We can still believe in God's sovereignty and we can still praise God, but the expression of it becomes quite different.

- If we subsequently reach a point where we are relieved from our trouble, it is natural to give thanks to God afresh for the specific relief we have experienced. Psalms of thanksgiving, such as Psalm 30 here, are the ones that fit such circumstances.

So this psalm tells an intriguing story, packed with emotion, and a little exaggeration, that reflects in microcosm the ups and downs of life. It tells us that joys and sorrows are equally part of the experience of living as God's people, and helps us to appreciate the different types of psalm that belong to different phases of the cycle of comfort, disruption and recovery. Wherever you are in that cycle right now, there will be a psalm that helps you to express it, whether a hymn, a lament or a thanksgiving.

Psalm 67

Psalm 67 has an interesting structure that can shape the way in which we examine it. So, first of all, look out for its symmetrical structure with corresponding elements in layers which focus in on the middle, indicating a central element that is primary. Verses 1–2 match verses 6–7 in describing land and blessing. Verse 3 matches verse 5 exactly, with identical words. And, so, verse 4 is central: the focal point of the psalm. Read the psalm through, bearing in mind that structure. Now let's examine each element.

The central element in verse 4 is an expression of praise: 'Let the nations be glad and sing for joy, for you [God] will judge the peoples with equity and guide the nations upon earth.' Praise in this psalm is declaring the truth that God is the ruler who cares for all people and ensures that justice is done. God rules justly, fairly, equitably, lifting up the humble and the downtrodden, and standing for them and fighting for them and ensuring that everyone is fairly treated. That is the sort of ruler that God is. To praise God, in this context, is to proclaim, 'This is the truth, this is the God that we believe in.'

Praise is the right attitude towards God, recognising that God is the supreme authority. God deserves our reverence and our awe. If we praise God by focusing on his worthiness and declaring his goodness, not only are we doing what is our duty, but we are also giving ourselves joy; it is our joy to praise God. Why? Because it gives us stability and security: it anchors us in the reality of God's goodness and God's faithfulness and God's dependability. The more we immerse ourselves in the truth of who God is, the more secure and stable we will be, because we will have confidence in God and will know ourselves loved by God. So praising God is good for us, in a fairly direct way; not only is it right and proper and dutiful, but it is what we need.

Can you see how the praise of God is expressed with a reason for that praise: 'for you judge the peoples with equity and guide the nations upon earth'? This pattern is almost always evident when God is praised in the psalms. The reason for praise is either to do with who God is or something that God has done. The recitation of God's praiseworthiness guards against idolatry; it ensures that God is worshipped as God truly is, not just some other idea that we have concocted for ourselves. It keeps us grounded in the truth.

The vision of praise in this psalm is an all-encompassing one, intending that *everyone* might praise God: 'Let the peoples praise you, O God, let all the peoples praise you' (v. 3, 5). These two verses are identical, forming a frame around the central element of verse 4 which gives the greater detail and reason for praise. Wouldn't it be great if everyone praised God? Wouldn't the world be a good place if everyone had a right attitude towards God? The praise of the psalmist is intended for other people to hear and be drawn into the same exuberant song of joy. How could we use this psalm so that other people 'hear' our praise of God and are drawn towards God's goodness?

The psalm also has an outer layer of matching frames. Look at how it begins and ends. 'May God be gracious to us and bless us and make his face to shine upon us, that your way may be known upon earth, your saving power among all nations' is the opening (vv. 1–2). Those two verses express the wish that God's salvation would become evident to all the people of the earth. It assumes that this may come about when God's face shines upon 'us' (God's people). Note that God is to be revealed as gracious: God's blessing and God's shining on people is not because of their merit.

The same themes are evident in the matching frame at the end of the psalm. 'The earth has yielded its increase; God, our God, has blessed us. May God continue to bless us; let all the ends of the earth revere him' (vv. 6–7). The mention of harvest suggests that this psalm might have been a harvest hymn, specifically written to express thanks and praise to the God whose goodness is evident in the provision of a harvest. So it is a prayer that the earth will yield its harvest, i.e. that we will have what we need.

C.S. Lewis described praise as the 'consummation' of the enjoyment of God. The joy in knowing and loving God is found in expressing our praise, and this psalm gives us a wonderful glimpse of how that can spread and be transformative.

Psalm 58

Have you ever felt a sense of indignation when you have seen people in power abusing their privilege by doing harm to others? Has a sense of anger been fuelled by your impotence to stop them and the sense that they can get away with whatever they want? Well, Psalm 58 is the prayer for you! Read it through with those kinds of feelings in mind.

The psalm opens with a pair of rhetorical questions addressed symbolically to the 'rulers' who abuse their power. Do they decree what is right? Do they judge people fairly? The context envisaged here is one where people's livelihoods and well-being depend on the 'decrees' and 'judgements' of the rulers. The kind of judgement in view is not about whether a person is innocent or guilty of a crime. Rather, it would be about ownership of property, rights to their harvest or restitution of something that has been taken from them. In a context of subsistence agricultural society, these are potentially matters of life and death. If someone in power claims one of your fields and takes it off you, how are you going to grow enough food to feed your family?

The implied answer of the opening rhetorical questions is 'No' but, just to be sure, the psalmist states it explicitly in verse 2. He accuses the rulers of 'wrongs' and 'violence'. We get a sense here of the frustration of seeming powerlessness in the face of evil. What can you do when those with the strength and the authority and the wealth take advantage of the weak and the poor?

The next few verses (vv. 3–5) offer an image of the wicked as snakes. They are poisonous and they are deaf, implying that they pay no heed to those who are telling them to do what is right. This is presented in terms of a snake that ignores the charmer: thus, a dangerous animal that defies attempts to control it or be put to any good purpose. We might wonder why these verses are included in the psalm. Who are they addressed to? Nobody explicitly, but presumably they are intended to be heard by anyone who is listening. Perhaps they offer a warning to anyone, whether they are a 'ruler' or not, to guard themselves against being deaf to good instruction. After all, self-righteousness can easily lead to harmful behaviour, even among those who are themselves downtrodden.

In verses 6–9, the psalmist makes his prayer to God to deal with the oppressive rulers. He does this in a series of quite shocking images. He wants them to have their teeth broken out, to vanish like water running away, to wither like trodden grass, or to dissolve into slime like a snail. Not for the faint-hearted! The apparent vengefulness and aggression of these images is quite shocking. Does this mean the psalmist is violent and vindictive? I think not, but we must read carefully and put ourselves into his context to really appreciate this.

We have already noted that the psalmist is in a desperate situation where his life and the life of his family are potentially at stake. He is a victim of other people's abuse and he is powerless to do anything about it. What does he want? Simply, he wants it to stop. He wants the situation to change so that he is no longer being abused or mistreated. So the first image says exactly this. Portraying the enemies as lions, he prays, 'Break their teeth.' In other words: 'Take away their means of doing harm.' The next image is of water that runs away: 'Let them vanish.' This implies nothing of their fate, only that they should be gone and the psalmist have some respite.

The strength of feeling that arises from the psalmist's desperation then spills over into images of wishing that his enemies were dead. However, I read this as an extension of the desire that they harm him no longer. It is probably based on his understanding of God's justice being active in people's lifetimes, such that extreme evil is punished by God through actual death. I don't think the psalmist is seriously thinking in a considered way that the enemies ought to die, but is perhaps assuming that God's way of breaking their power will be by ending their lives.

As we have noted previously, this is particularly apparent when we notice that the psalmist is not taking the matter into his own hands. He is not intending to do any harm to his enemies, nor is he calling upon anyone else to do so. Rather, he is relying entirely on God to protect him and help him, and he assumes that perhaps this might involve God bringing the evildoers to their end if that is the only way of stopping them.

The fundamental idea of justice – of the righteous and the weak being vindicated against the wicked and the powerful – is all the more apparent in the closing verses (vv. 10–11). The rejoicing of the righteous will be because of the reassurance that God does honour them and judges justly. This will come about when they 'see vengeance done', crucially not when they enact vengeance but when they see God enact it.

The gory image of 'bathing their feet in the blood of the wicked' might seem inappropriate for the prayer of a 'righteous' person, but, in reality, is simply another way of looking forward to the wicked meeting their judgement, along with a presumption that this might well involve their death. It is almost certainly not literal, but a figure of speech not unlike the modern idiom of saying that we will 'dance on someone's grave'.

So, to sum up, we need to think of someone who is in extreme life-threatening adversity in order to appreciate this psalm. Think of extreme persistent abuse or bullying; think of people forced from their homeland by extreme violence; think of those experiencing ethnic cleansing at the hands of an army. In such circumstances, this psalm offers a way of their crying out to God, 'Please stop them! Stop these evil people – make them go away!' And it connects with and expresses the most visceral emotions that inevitably are borne in such adversity, and which causes the victims to say, 'I would be glad if my oppressors were dead.' Yet the prayer is that God will respond;

the psalmist relinquishes any personal right or claim to retribution. The matter is left in God's hands.

For most, if not all, of us, I would hope that we will never have cause to pray this psalm in relation to real human enemies. However, we do read about situations in the world where people are faced with evil oppressive rulers, and we could pray this psalm on their behalf. In doing so, we must acknowledge that a Christian understanding is that God's judgement is reserved for the end of the age, and so we might not have such a strong expectation that it will be evident in our lifetimes.

Nevertheless, God's concern for justice is no less than before and it is right that we should cry out to God for justice. On a personal level, you might face circumstances when you are completely overpowered, not by specific people but by a disease or by overwhelming circumstances such as debt. At such times, you could use this psalm as your own prayer for God to 'break the teeth' of that which overpowers you, in the hope that you may rejoice when it is gone.

Psalm 48

Psalm 48 is an all-out, unambiguous celebration of the city of Jerusalem. The city is described as 'the joy of all the earth' (v. 2) in an exuberant claim about its place in the world. Verses 4–8 briefly refer to a particular context for the psalm, which is that other nations made an attack on Jerusalem but were repelled. This possibly originates in the actual assault on the city by the Assyrians, around 701BC. However, the precise details of that are not too significant for our own reading of the psalm, as we shall see shortly.

The celebration of Jerusalem and its significance in Israelite thinking are rooted in its being the location of both the king (vv. 1–2) and the temple (vv. 9–11), where God can be known and worshipped. These two aspects lead to a confidence in the security and steadfastness of the city, which is the subject of the psalm's conclusion (vv. 12–14).

What do you think about when you read or hear anything about 'Jerusalem'? There are actually quite a lot of possibilities. The ancient city of Jerusalem that the psalmist had in mind is only one of those possibilities. Even if we do think about the ancient city, it does not mean the same to us as it meant to the psalmist. Therefore, this psalm provides us with a useful case study for exploring the variety of ways in which we can interpret the psalms and apply them to our own situation.

Let's begin with thinking about *the actual ancient city of Jerusalem*, as the psalmist had in mind when the psalm was written. There are descriptions elsewhere in the Bible of the magnificence of the king's palace and the temple. These breathtaking structures would have inspired awe in the grandeur of God. Similarly, the walls, towers and ramparts of the city could foster confidence in the shelter and protection that the city could provide, and this acted as a sort of 'visual aid' to enable the psalmist to grasp the idea of God being a defensive shield, as described in verse 3.

Jerusalem had been established as the centre of the kingdom of Israel and as the one place where God could rightly be worshipped. Therefore, it represented to the psalmist God's previous victories, and the permanence of the settlement in the promised land, itself a gift of God. All these ideas combine to allow us to reflect on the ancient city of Jerusalem as the psalmist knew and understood it, to speak to us of God's faithfulness and invincibility.

In a Christian context, Jerusalem as a physical location is far less significant than it was for the ancient psalmist. God's people are no longer ruled by a human king, but by Jesus, the King of kings; and God's presence is no longer limited to the Jerusalem temple, but is active by the Holy Spirit in the lives of all believers, who are temples of God's Spirit. However, 'Jerusalem' as a concept or an image still has resonance as *a symbolic way of describing the church*, the community of God's people.

This symbolic interpretation of 'Jerusalem' is used in the New Testament, where the writer of the letter to the Hebrews describes Christians as having 'come to Mount Zion and to the city of the living God, the heavenly Jerusalem' (Hebrews 12:22). Thus 'Jerusalem' may be read as symbolising a spiritual community of believers. Read this way, the psalm is a celebration of the church and of God's presence within the church. It allows us to meditate on the security that God's presence provides and the permanence of our status as members of God's kingdom. It also offers the sobering reminder that we may experience the assaults of those 'foreign' powers that oppose God's purposes, although such powers can never ultimately prevail.

An example of the symbolic reading of 'Jerusalem' as the church is John Newton's hymn 'Glorious things of thee are spoken, Zion, city of our God'. (Zion is an alternative name for Jerusalem.) It is particularly evident in the line 'Saviour, if of Zion's city, I through grace a member am', leading to the conclusion: 'Solid joys and lasting treasure, none but Zion's children know'.

The symbolic reading of 'Jerusalem' is developed further in the New Testament where it speaks of the 'New Jerusalem' (Revelation 3:12; 21:2, 10) or 'heavenly city'. These instances invoke the idea of *the renewal of all creation at the end of the age*. The perfect enactment of God's rule is understood to create an extraordinary restoration and a whole new world order. This is depicted as a 'New Jerusalem' which comes 'from heaven' and so is more full of God's presence than the world has ever been before. This is the 'Jerusalem' which is to come, our eternal hope.

If you read the psalm with this sense of 'Jerusalem' in mind, the psalm becomes a meditation on the Christian hope for a better future, for an eternal home that is completely secure and completely filled with the presence of God and of Jesus Christ the King of kings. This future-oriented reading particularly resonates with the conclusion to the psalm, which speaks of 'the next generation' and God's eternal nature.

Thus, you can read Psalm 48 with three different interpretations of 'Jerusalem', allowing you to make different applications of its celebration of God's sovereignty and consequent security for God's people. You can read through the eyes of the psalmist and consider the ancient city of Jerusalem; you can apply it to a contemporary context and ponder the status of the Christian church; and you can look forward in hope and meditate on God's perfect kingdom which is yet to come.

Maybe have a go at all three ways of reading and see what different ideas take prominence. Doing so takes full advantage of the richness and depth of this psalm and can encourage you to apply similar principles to many other psalms too.

8

And finally... famous openings

The psalms have been the staple diet of Jewish and Christian prayer for many centuries, so reading them connects us into that great faith tradition of all who have gone before us. In using the psalms, we stand alongside all those who have walked before us, and are reminded that we are part of that great company of heaven, serving and worshipping our God and King forever.

Down the centuries, some psalms have found particular resonance in specific contexts, such that they become closely associated with those contexts. In these cases, the sense of connection with the community of faith in the past is even stronger. Here are a few examples of openings to psalms that have been particularly well known or associated with specific events.

Psalm 122 opens with:

> I was glad when they said to me,
>   'Let us go to the house of the Lord!'
> Our feet are standing,
>   within your gates, O Jerusalem.
>
> PSALM 122:1–2

This is often assumed to be a psalm of pilgrimage, used as the pilgrims arrived at Jerusalem for a festival and full of joy to be among the gathering people. Put yourself into this situation and imagine how it felt to be part of such a great gathering of people. Ponder the reasons for the psalmist being so glad: perhaps grateful for a safe journey, or anticipating the feast, or excited by the prospect of seeing again the splendour of the temple, or lifted up in spirit as he remembers the stories of the exodus and conquest that established the people in the land. In doing so, you can be caught up in the experience of the psalmist, and marvel that the community of faith spans an unbroken chain of 2,500 years from that pilgrim in Jerusalem to yourself today.

The psalm continues with the well-known prayer for the peace of Jerusalem, concluding:

For the sake of my relatives and friends
  I will say, 'Peace be within you.'
For the sake of the house of the Lord our God,
  I will seek your good.

PSALM 122:8–9

Here, we enter the psalmist's heart and those things which are most dear to him: relatives, friends and the house of God. So too we can use the psalm to pray for those dear to us, knowing that we share the same concerns as our forebears in faith. As we read the psalm, the psalmist's history becomes our history.

Psalm 130 is an incredibly evocative psalm of lament which begins with a haunting cry:

Out of the depths I cry to you, O Lord.
  Lord, hear my voice!
Let your ears be attentive
  to the voice of my supplications!
If you, O Lord, should mark iniquities,
  Lord, who could stand?

PSALM 130:1–3

Psalm 130 has been a source of spiritual nourishment to many in times of great trouble. The open and evocative language of 'depths' lends itself to interpretation in all manner of ways according to particular circumstances. St Augustine wrote words from this psalm on the wall when he was in his final days. John Wesley had his experience of conversion on the same day as hearing the psalm sung in St Paul's Cathedral. His response to the psalm was preparatory to the marvellous work of grace that God was to do in his life within the following few hours.

The significance of the psalm goes far beyond giving expression to one person's feelings. As you read it, you are joined with Augustine and Wesley and countless other believers who have walked the road of suffering or guilt or seemingly incessant waiting. You can be reassured that you are not alone. You find common ground with those who have gone before, and endured their adversity, remaining true to their faith, placing their hope in God.

Finally, perhaps the most potent example of all comes from Psalm 22, the 'cry of dereliction' that Jesus used on the cross:

> My God, my God, why have you forsaken me?
> Why are you so far from helping me, from the words of my groaning?

PSALM 22:1–4

The original context of the psalm is obscure, but Christian reading of the psalm is inevitably influenced by Jesus' quoting it on the cross and his own identification with the psalmist. Although, in the gospels, Jesus is recorded as quoting only this opening verse, it is often supposed that it indicates that he prayed the whole psalm while on the cross.

Much of the imagery of the psalm, describing the affliction and torment of the psalmist, finds fresh relevance in the events of Jesus' crucifixion. The scoffing crowds, the physical trauma and the loss of clothes that become gambling prizes: these all find fresh resonance and significance in the events of the crucifixion. So much so that for anyone familiar with the story, it becomes very difficult to read the psalm without interpreting it in the light of the experience of Jesus.

By hearing the voice of Jesus in the psalm, you can read it as the expression of the one who fulfils the life of ancient Israel and who represents the church of all those who follow him. Jesus, in appropriating the psalm to the circumstances of his passion, is identifying himself with the suffering and crying out to God of all humanity. You can therefore bring your own suffering and trauma into the light of the psalm in order to find fresh perspective on it, just as, by praying the psalm on the cross, Jesus saw his own circumstances through the lens of the psalmist's experience.

So, to finish where we started: why read the psalms? Because our Lord Jesus Christ did. They nourished his relationship with God the Father and so may they nourish yours too.

Questions for reflection and discussion

1. What has surprised you about the psalms?
2. What have you learned from the psalms about how God's people relate to God? About God?
3. How has reading the psalms shaped your spiritual life? How has it shaped your prayer life?
4. How would you encourage others to read Psalms?
5. If you had to choose the three most important psalms, what would they be? Why?
6. If this book were not in the Bible, how would you argue for its inclusion?
7. What aspects of modern living can be related to the situations addressed in the psalms?
8. How could the psalms be used to reach out to people with the gospel message?